SKETCHES
in pen & ink and watercolor
by Serge Hollerbach

To Milton and Gloria
Bert —

fondly,
Serge Hollerbach
9/15/87

Library of Congress Cataloging In-Publication Data
NC 139.G614A4   1987   741.973   87-15242

Design: Serge Hollerbach
Photography: Studio Nine
Printed by Reproduction Typographers and Printers

The art of sketching involves the ability to perceive and express qualities that exist beyond what most of us see as only the ordinary. In this book of sketches and watercolors, Serge Hollerbach demonstrates his ability to see beyond the obvious and then give expression to what he feels. He shares with us a world we are all familiar with — but through these crisp and incisive images we see with new eyes our old world.

Serge Hollerbach was born in Russia in 1923 and was educated at the Academy of Fine Arts in Munich, West Germany from 1946-1949. To pay for his tuition and support himself, Hollerbach worked as a sketch artist at the American Red Cross club doing quick portraits of American soldiers. This experience marked the beginning of his life-long interest in sketching, which he continues to practice today, along with his more ambitious figurative work in oils and acrylics.

Today Hollerbach is rarely without his sketch pad. The life of the city attracts his attention everywhere. Through his sketches we see ourselves — we feel the joy and sadness and loneliness, the humor, fatigue and energy that make up the human condition. In these sketches, Hollerbach captures the character and movement of his subject with a minimum of lines and washes of color. The art of Serge Hollerbach is compassionate and at the same time committed — yet he still allows us to share an occasional laugh with one another.

Newman and Saunders Galleries are pleased to represent Serge Hollerbach and present a book of his sketches and watercolors, done over the past twenty years in the United States and Europe.

Drew C. Saunders
September 1987

pen and ink   6″ × 8″

Sketching is my love and my favorite pastime. It is also an integral part of all of my artistic activities. I can even speak of a "lure" for sketching — an addiction of sorts — that possesses an artist in the same way that hunting possesses a hunter or fishing a fisherman. Why? What is it actually? Have people become a game for a sketch artist? In a way — yes. But it is not so simple. When you draw gesture, follow the lines of a profile or depict people engaged in some sort of activity — you meet them. Because of your involvement, you participate and share with them whatever they are doing. When observing the shapes, expressions, manners, clothing or certain peculiarities of body movement, the artist comes to know his subject almost intimately. This intimacy is not unlike the one that binds us to a person we love. From the moment we are born we are learning about the world around us. We begin by seeing and touching and experiencing through our senses until we can later touch the world with our pencil or charcoal or brush. We are also creating in our art an eternity of images — a paradise where nothing ever changes and no one ever dies. All of this keeps the artist spellbound and provides him with a limitless source of inspiration and discovery. The following pages record my fascination with people in their everyday activities. I have included some observations and impressions at times because I find everything from amusement to endearment to sadness in them.

pen and brown ink 10½″ × 7½″

The easiest thing is to sketch people as they sleep — they don't move. But this is not the only advantage. A person sleeping is interesting because his face and body expresses a certain inward concentration — a "looking inside of oneself." We can almost see him dreaming, and if we know the vocabulary we can interpret the body language. The awkwardness of their pose shows both their strengths and vulnerabilities. The expressions of intelligent or pleasant people can change and become silly or sour. Portrait painters know this and try constantly to keep the sitter amused or interested so that the facial expression remains natural and lively. Sketching, however, is a more intimate form of art and these "unofficial" views of people are perfectly legitimate.

pen and brown ink 10½″ × 8″

pen and brown ink 8″ × 8″

pen and brown ink 11½″ × 7½″

Good sandwich, pen and ink 8″ × 5″

Eating is another human activity that offers the artist an interesting field of observation. We see two poles — the mouth and the hand that carries food to it. There is an imaginary trajectory that creates tension between the two poles that has to be expressed. There are also the elements of the way a person holds the fork or spoon, the fingers and facial expression and the whole posture of the body that need expression as well. While eating alone in a restaurant I make it a habit to carry with me a small sketchbook that resembles a book so as to remain inconspicuous. After ordering there is plenty of time to look around and find a variety of interesting people to sketch. Note: Sketching works best without cocktails preceding the meal — or at least before the cocktail has any effect on you. Only Toulouse-Lautrec seemed to be immune from it. I couldn't resist the temptation to give each drawing a caption — my own interpretation of their emotions while eating.

Surprised, pen and ink 8″ × 5″

Eager, pen and ink 8″ × 5″

Hungry, pen and ink 8″ × 5″

Enough, pen and ink 8″ × 5″

pen and brown ink   10½″ × 7½″

People reading offer a wide range of expressions — face and body of equal importance.

pen and brown ink 11″ × 8″

pen and brown ink 12″ × 8½″

pen and brown ink 10½″ × 8″

In the train Milano — Marseille, 1986   pen, ink and watercolor   10½″ × 8″

Man reading, Vienna, 1983   pen, ink and watercolor   11½″ × 8″

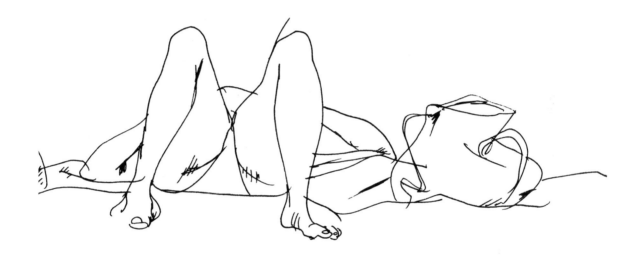

Summer weather brings people to the beach. Since life began in the oceans, this migration of man to the sea is somehow primordial: beasts returning to their beginnings. Being a poor swimmer I return after a quick dip to my beach chair not only to enjoy the air and sun and sea, but to observe my fellow human beings as they swim and play and relax. I must confess that a comparison with a colony of pink and golden seals in colorful swimwear comes to mind. Far from being derogatory, this similarity is for me very touching — human in the nicest possible way. "Here we are," I keep thinking, "warming our bodies in the rays of an ancient star that gave life to all things." The sun cleanses and purifies us — not only our bodies but our souls, too. We rejoin the great family of living things, leaving behind our egos and intellect and reverting back to our more simple selves. Sketching people at the beach is a unique experience for an artist. He sees the shapes of people as organic forms, almost abstract yet full of human expression. Some bodies are fragile and vulnerable, others robust and assertive. Sometimes there are interesting combinations: a shy, childlike face and a mature, aggressive body — or a wise and even world-weary face and a tender, youthful body. Hands, feet, hair, gestures — everything is fascinating and even slightly amusing; for we tend to smile warmly when we see something that touches our heart.

Some of the sketches have been done on beaches in southern France and elsewhere in Europe, where topless and nude bathing and sunbathing is permitted or tolerated. The more revealing drawings and watercolors were done not on the spot, but later in the hotel room.

17

pen and brown ink 10″ × 8″

pen and brown ink 10″ × 7½″

Children's gestures — their awkwardness, grace and innocence — is what I am always trying to catch.

Sunbathers in the park, 1985 pen, ink and watercolor 10″ × 8″

Girl reading, 1986 watercolor 9½″ × 7½″

Two sunbathers, 1981 pen, ink and watercolor 10½″ × 8″

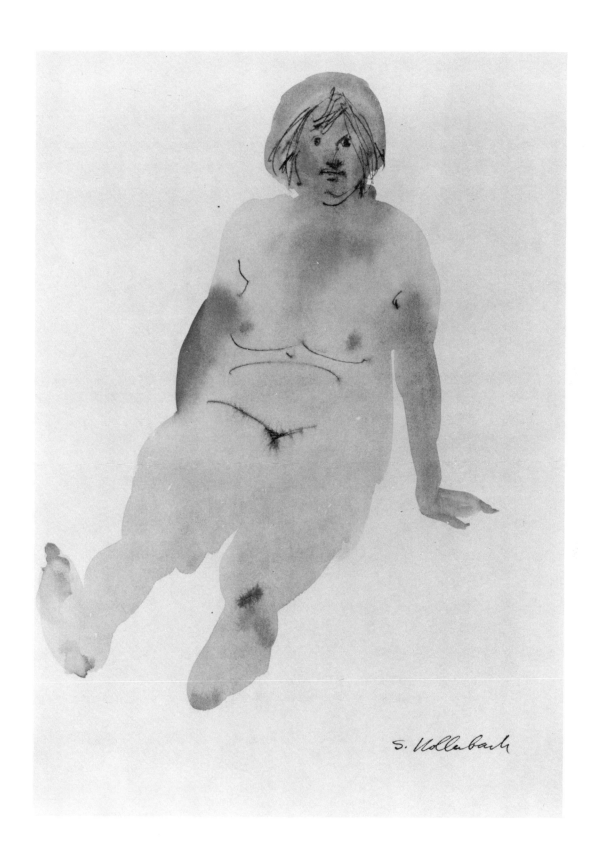

S. Wollerbach

Nude bather, 1983 pen, ink and watercolor 10½″ × 8″

23

Beach shower, 1981 pen, ink and watercolor 11″ × 8″

24

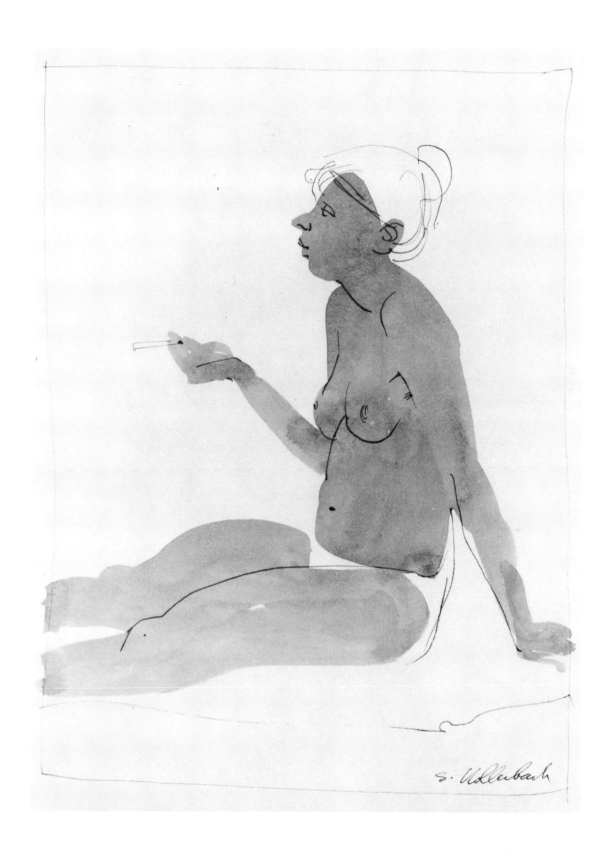

Girl with a cigarette, 1981 pen, ink and watercolor 10½" × 8"

Cote d'Azur bathers, 1981 pen, ink and watercolor 10½″ × 8″

Candlewood Lake beach, 1985 pen, ink and watercolor 11" × 8"

Flemings Hotel, London, 1980 pen, ink and watercolor 11″ × 8″

Painting the interior of my hotel room while traveling has become a habit for me — almost like scribbling on the wall "Such and such was here." While staying overnight in a hotel room you establish a close, almost intimate relationship with your surroundings. It is in some ways similar to knowing a woman in the Biblical sense. You become familiar with the light, sounds, textures and smells of your dwelling. Life outside its walls is different from that at home and it makes you feel more involved and even closer to your temporary quarters. Glancing through these sketches is like looking through a family album and recalling the good times and places. The bed in this sketch is not made — it is more interesting with all the lines and folds of the blankets and sheets.

426   Hotel Schneider, Wien   Aug. 8 1983

Hotel Schneider, Vienna, 1983 pen, ink and watercolor 11″ × 8″

Street scene, 1986   pen and ink 14″ × 17″

And then there is the street, which is the main stage of the human theatre. At home or while traveling abroad, I always try to record my impressions of the locale — people in their surroundings with their children and pets. Sketching on the spot is often difficult if not impossible, so I try to memorize gesture, shape, and contrast and then to reconstruct them later in pen and ink, wash and watercolor.

A sketchbook is a diary, a personal statement and a record of things observed.

Rainy day, 1985 pen, ink and watercolor 10½" × 8"

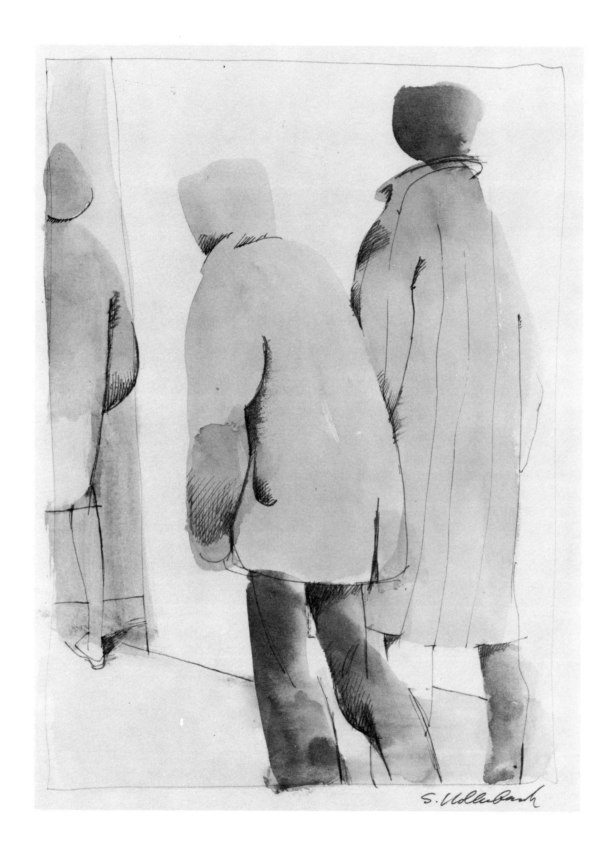

Figures in winter, 1983 pen, ink and watercolor 10½″ × 8″

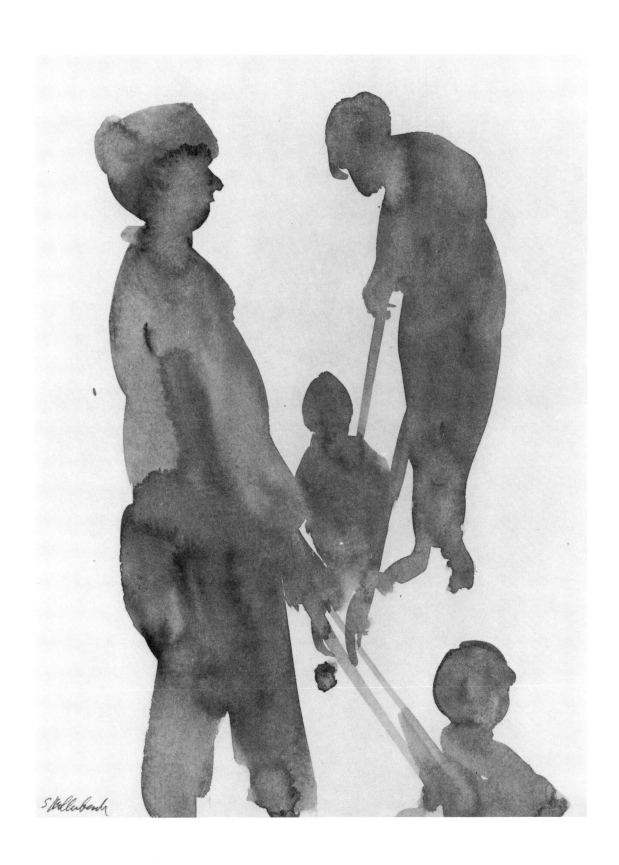

Women and children, 1984 watercolor 10½″ × 8″

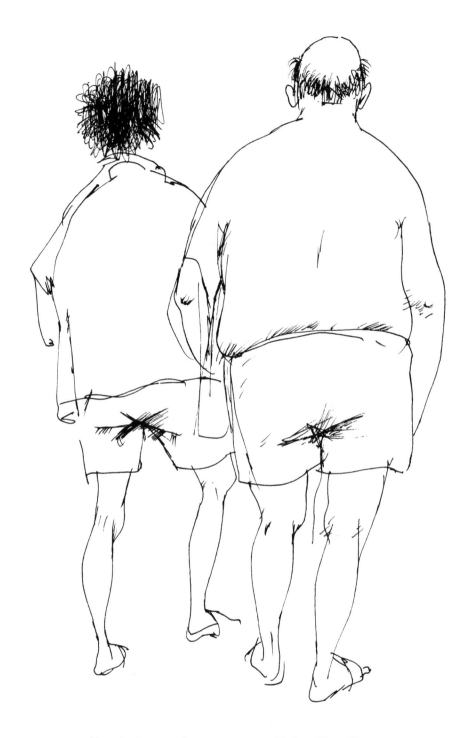

Vacationing couple, 1982 pen and ink 11″ × 8″

Couples — young, old, bound by love or habit, have a unity that is expressive and direct and always interesting to sketch.

Many people in my sketches are seen from the back. The reason is obvious — I sketch them when they cannot see me. But I also believe that the back view has just as much character as the front view. The human body reveals from the back its weight, its build, and its posture more clearly, undisturbed by face, breasts, lapels, buttons, etc.

Young couple, 1982 pen and ink 11″ × 8″

Man and dog, 1981 pen and ink 11″ × 8″

Sketching sleeping dogs is easy. You may get a drawing good enough for a family album or a calendar, but only a sketch of a dog in action or, at least, in its waking moments will have certain spirit and humor. Here are some of my attempts to see man's best friend in his everyday activities.

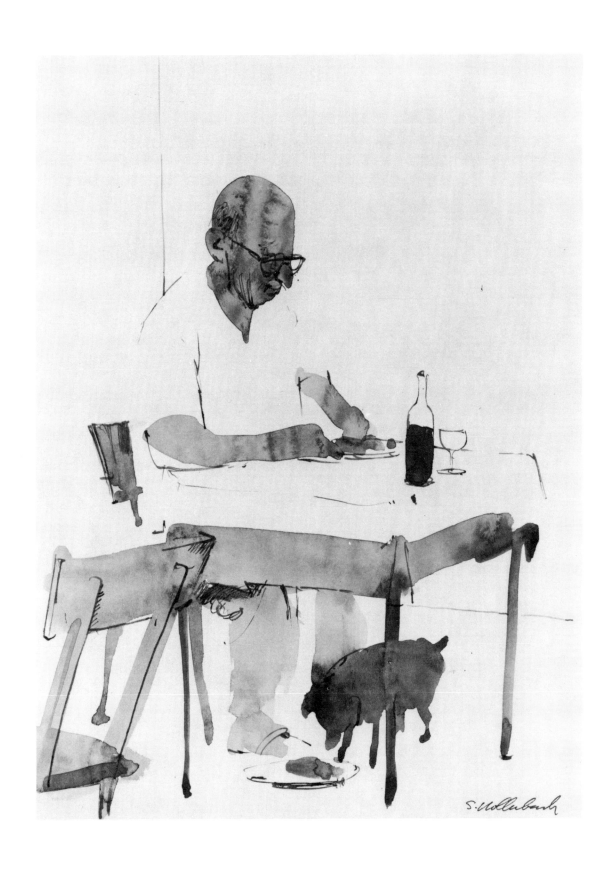

Frenchman dining, 1985 pen, ink and watercolor 10½″ × 8″

37

Morning walk, 1983 watercolor 10½″ × 8″

Frenchman with dachshund, 1985 watercolor 10½" × 8"

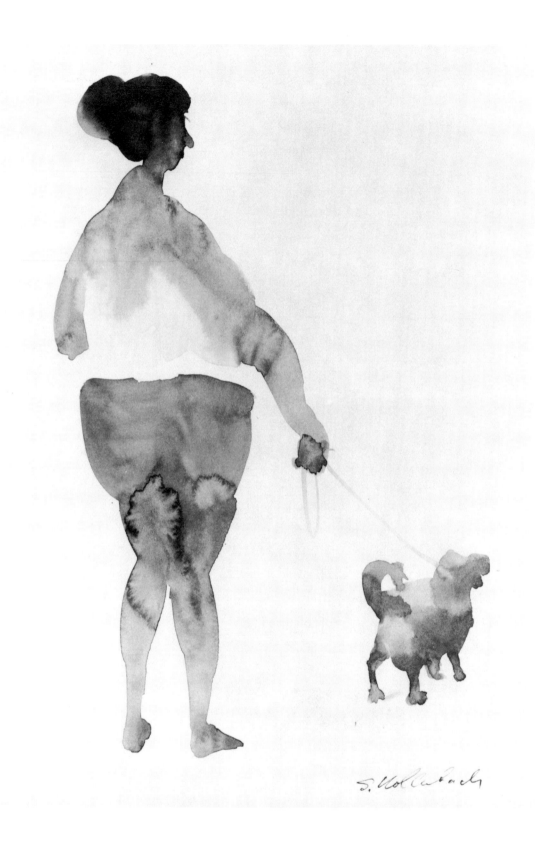

Woman and dog, 1983 watercolor 10½″ × 8″

Frenchman and his dog, 1985 pen, ink and watercolor 10½ × 7½″

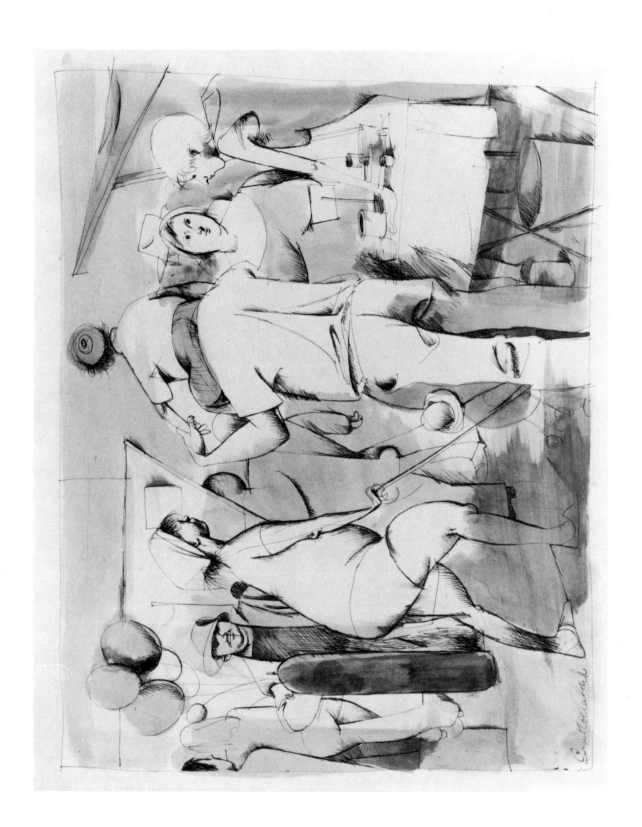

Street fair, 1983 pen, ink and wash 14″ × 17″

Summer in the park, 1983   pen, ink and wash 14" × 17"

Three figures, 1986 pen and colored inks 12″ × 10″

Cyclist, 1984 watercolor 10½″ × 8″

45

Old man, 1985 pen, ink and watercolor 10″ × 7½″

Mother and child, 1986 watercolor 10½″ × 7½″

Two girls, 1983 watercolor 11½″ × 8½″

48

Street scene, 1986 pen, ink and watercolor 10½″ × 8″

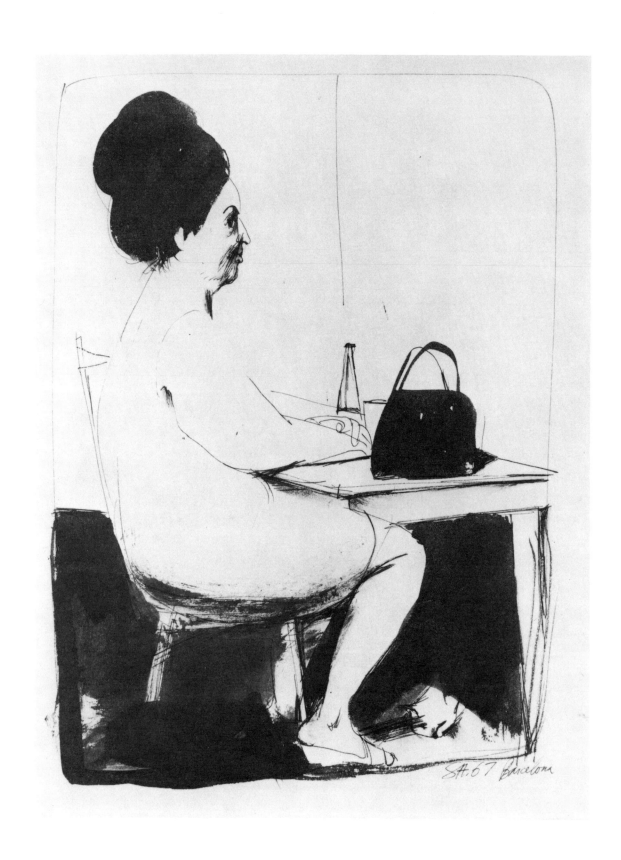

Prostitute in Barcelona, Spain, 1967 pen and brush 14″ × 10″

Butcher in Lisbon, Portugal, 1968 pen, ink and brush 14″ × 10½″

Fisherwomen in Nazare, Portugal, 1968 ink and wash 14″ × 10½″

Portuguese fishermen, Nazare, Portugal, 1968 pen, ink and brush 14″ × 10½″

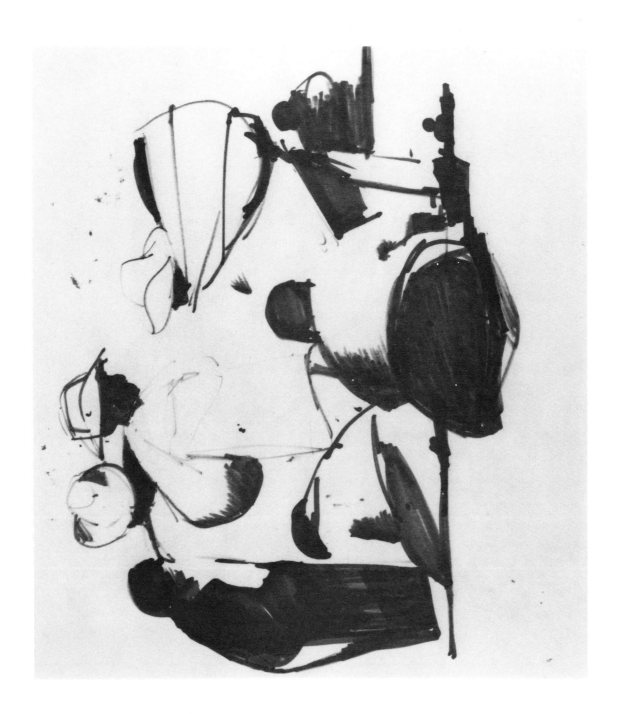

Mexican bazaar, 1965 felt pen and brown ink 9″ × 10½″

Mexican couple, 1980 pen, ink and watercolor 11″ × 8″

Mexican street, 1980 pen, ink and watercolor 8″ × 11½″

Mexican women, 1965 felt pen and brown ink 14″ × 10″

Amsterdam

S. Hollenbach

View from the window, Amsterdam, 1976 pen, ink and watercolor 11½" × 8"

Two priests in Patmos, Greece, 1974 pen, ink and brush 17″ × 14″

Mosque on the island of Kos, Greece, 1974 ink and brush 17" × 14"

Cafe in Mykonos, Greece, 1969 pen, ink and brush 14″ × 10½″

61

Couple in Mykonos, Greece, 1974 ink and brush 17″ × 14″

Donkey, Greece, 1969 pen, ink and brush 14″ × 10½″

Boats in Kos, Greece, 1974 ink, brush and wash 10¾" × 14"

Turkish couple with sheep, Bodrum, Turkey, 1974 pen, ink and wash 14″ × 10¾″

Church in Mykonos, Greece, 1974 pen, ink and wash 14″ × 10¾″

French restaurant, 1983 pen, ink and watercolor 10″ × 8″

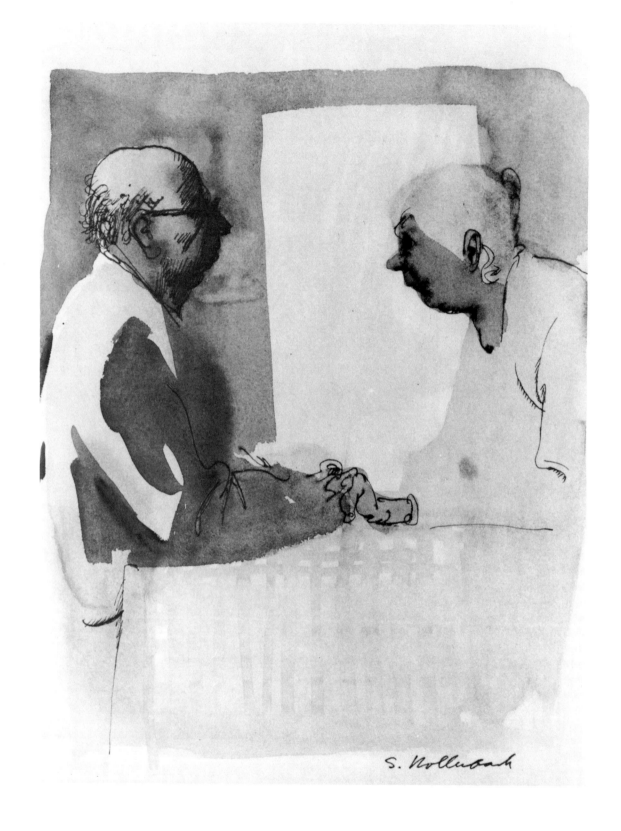

Old couple, 1985 pen, ink and watercolor 10½″ × 8″

pen & ink 6″ × 6″

This drawing, made in one of the numerous sketch classes around town, expresses self-doubt — a feeling all too common to artists. Yet the joy of sketching should be stronger than any other feeling. However necessary and justified self-criticism is, it should never hinder or frighten. It has been said that only fools and wise men are happy. To be a happy fool in art is a rewarding experience.

SERGE HOLLERBACH

Born: 1923, in Pushkin, Russia.

Studied: Munich Academy of Fine Arts
Munich, West Germany, 1946-1949.
Art Students League, New York City, 1951.
American Art School, New York City, 1952.

Member: National Academy of Design (Academician)
American Watercolor Society
Allied Artists of America
Audubon Artists
National Society of Painters in Casein and Acrylic

Exhibited: American Academy of Arts and Letters
National Academy of Design
National Arts Club
Butler Institute of American Art
Drawings USA
Watercolor USA

Work In: Yale University Art Gallery, New Haven, CT
Thomas P. Whitney Collection
St. Paul Gallery of Art, MN
Bridgeport Museum, Bridgeport, CT
Georgia Museum of Art, Athens, GA
Seton Hall University Art Gallery, So. Orange, NJ
Norfolk Museum of Arts and Sciences
Oklahoma Museum of Art
Bergen Museum of Art and Science, NJ
Butler Institute of American Art
National Academy of Design
Philbrook Art Center, Tulsa, OK
University of Kentucky Art Museum